A
RESTLESS
EVIL

A
RESTLESS
EVIL

DENTAL DANGER

ZACHARY WAYNE LAVENDER

XULON PRESS

Xulon Press
2301 Lucien Way #415
Maitland, FL 32751
407.339.4217
www.xulonpress.com

Paperback ISBN-13: 978-1-66286-710-1
Ebook ISBN-13: 978-1-66286-711-8

DEDICATION

To the Church Universal,

"If anyone thinks he is religious and does not *bridle* his tongue
but deceives his *heart*, this person's religion is worthless."
—James 1:26

"If we wholeheartedly desire to tame our tongue, we
must first deal with the condition of our *hearts*."
—Zachary Wayne Lavender

"What are we '*feeding*' our *hearts?*"
—Zachary Wayne Lavender

"A good man brings good things out of the good stored up in his
heart. And the evil man brings evil things out of the evil stored
up in his *heart*. For the *mouth speaks* what the *heart is full of.*"
—Luke 6:45

FOREWORD

It was the most beautiful time of the year! Christmas 2018 at Lifeline Church in Cicero, Illinois. The children were to sing a couple of selections. This usually meant three to seven minutes of auditory torture! A lack of aptitude, training, and rehearsal time was usually the culprit. Children's choirs were typically not well-trained or disciplined. The adults encourage the children by sprinkling in the cursory "Amen" or "Take your time." This, dear reader, was nothing like that! Within seconds our mouths flung wide open like the Red Sea. The children were phenomenal! Mr. Lavender had them singing in perfect pitch, and their timing and rhythm were impeccable! We were astounded!

Shortly before the pandemic arrived, there had been a shocking string of pastor suicides. Mr. Lavender spoke before a group of well-known pastors. As he addressed the topic of betrayal and suicide, the faces of these men and women of God softened and brightened as he exegeted the issues masterfully. At this symposium, we learned about Mr. Lavender's first work, *Victim of Circumstance*. Upon completing this book, we had a new favorite author who has transformed our lives!

We find Mr. Lavender's writing and teaching style immersive yet straightforward. Like watching a fish in water, you see its genius, calling, and purpose. So likewise, you will be immersed in your calling, purpose, and genius when you read his literary works. However, remember to watch your tongue.

Ernest and Simone Henton

FOREWORD

Zachary Lavender turned a personal conviction regarding his response to a stressful situation into powerful teaching about the unbridled power of an unruly tongue. He is a gifted musician and teacher with a heart to serve God and share with others what he has learned in his devotion and study on a subject that I dare say pertains to every person with the ability to speak.

Mr. Lavender uses the Word of God to carefully examine the power of the tongue and its connection to what is deep within a person's heart. Then, he explains why we have such a hard time controlling the things we say and to help us make better life-giving choices.

His teaching is crystal clear and compelling and, if taken to heart, will improve the quality of our lives and the lives of those around us. Thank you, Zachary, for taking the time to pen this simple yet powerful teaching on a *restless evil.*

Minister Debora Barr
All Things New Ministry

CONTENTS

INTRODUCTION

"Sticks and stones may break my bones, but words will never hurt me."
—Alexander William Kinglake

I wish I had been compensated for the many times another child said, *"Sticks and stones may break my bones, but words will never hurt me."* I've often said to other children, *"Sticks and stones may break my bones, but words will never hurt me,"* at this stage of my life, I could be a multibillionaire. However, that's not the case yet. Now that I'm older and a little wiser, I understand the meaning and context behind this adage. The latter part of this axiom is *"further from the truth."* If someone wants to harm you with sticks and stones, it will likely cause more damage than *"breaking your bones."* So the question is, *"What would make someone attack another person with sticks and stones?"* The idea of sticks and stones is to cause harm, not realizing the words spoken are causing much more than damage. *Words have power, weight, the potential to hurt, and the potential to help and heal.* What we say to others can damage their spirit, emotions, feelings, and self-esteem. Words can hurt, help, or heal mentally, physically, emotionally, or spiritually. Ultimately, the words we speak can cause great forest fires!

ONLY YOU CAN PREVENT FOREST FIRES

"It only takes a spark, remember, to set off a forest fire. A careless or wrongly placed word out of your mouth can do that."
(James 3:5–6)

In 1944 a nationwide campaign was introduced featuring Smokey the Bear, along with the slogan, "*Smokey says–Care will prevent nine out of ten forest fires.*" Later the slogan was modified to, "*Remember . . . only* you *can prevent forest fires.*" Smokey Bear (also known as Smokey the Bear) was a mascot of the United States Forest Service. His character's role was to bring awareness and teach others about the danger of forest fires. The objective was to educate local communities about the threat of forest fires and how they could prevent them from starting. The government later began making advertisements about the importance of fire safety.

What Is Fire?

Fire is a chemical reaction that disperses light and heat, which causes flames to occur to produce small particles of combustible materials that are heated to travel upward. Fire is one of God's most unique gifts to mankind. He created fire to do various things. With it, we can cook, destroy garbage, generate heat for our homes, and make metal tools. There are several other uses of fire.

The Bible tells us in James 3:5 that the *tongue* is likened to "*a fire.*" Which implies the tongue can be constructive and destructive.

How Can Fire Be Constructive?

- Fire gave humans the first form of portable light and heat
- Fire provides us with the ability to cook food
- Fire gives us the ability to forge metal tools
- Fire provides us with the ability to form pottery
- Fire gives us the ability to harden bricks
- Fire cleans the forest floor of debris

How Can Fire Be Destructive?

- Fire can destroy homes and possessions
- Fire can reduce an entire forest to a pile of ash

- Fire kills more people every year than any other force of nature
- Fire can destroy wildlife habitation
- Fire can pollute the air with emissions harmful to human health

What our tongues unleash reveals the very nature of the human heart. Matthew 12:35 says,

> "A good man out of the good treasure, of his heart, brings forth good things, and an evil man out of the evil treasure brings forth evil things."

In and of ourselves, we're not capable of "taming our tongue." One might ask, "Why is it difficult to tame our tongues?" When Adam sinned, his rebellion was imputed to mankind, so whether we believe it or not, all mankind was born with an evil, sinful nature and a wicked heart (Rom. 3:10–18). Various dysfunctions within each of us include jealousy, malice, hatred, greed, and envy. The tongue grips hold other destructive behaviors and lashes out, with Satan at the helm.

Consider this: How much time, thought, and care have you given to choosing your words? How much effort, energy, and endeavor have you devoted to speaking words of life and encouragement? Our mouths are like loaded guns. Once the pellets are released from the chamber, you cannot reach out and retrieve them. The bullets are out of the gun, and they cause much damage and, sometimes, death. There's only one way to prevent the pellets from leaving the barrel. *Don't shoot the weapon!* In other words, don't speak words that can cause damage, destruction, and death. As I studied this topic of the tongue, my convictions were heavy yet beneficial for my spiritual growth and maturity. I pray this book will help you understand the importance of the words you speak and their connection to the words you live.

Zachary Wayne Lavender
Author

Chapter One

WHAT'S THE RUSH?

A s a child, my mother was infamous for teaching such profound lessons as *"Be very careful what you say to others because you don't know what they're dealing with."* Her words and lessons are the subjects expounded in James 3:1–12. What an important and vital subject this is, and how much we need to heed God's Word regarding the right and wrong use of the tongue. The fact of the matter regarding our speech is that God created it to help and not hurt others. And if we misuse the tongue to bring sadness, sorrow, and suffering to others, we will be hindering others' testimony of the Lord Jesus Christ. Throughout his letter, James has much to say to the church about this matter, and it may suggest there was a problem. So James brilliantly shows us that the tongue of a Christian is a clear indicator of the Christian's spiritual growth, maturity, and integrity. Our speech reveals what kind of Christian we are and the condition of our hearts. What's in our hearts, our mouths will divulge.

> *My brethren, let not many of you become teachers, my brethren, knowing that as such, we will incur a stricter judgment. For we all stumble in many ways. If anyone does not stumble in what he says, he is a perfect man, able to bridle the whole body as well. Now, if we put the bits into the horses' mouths so that they will obey us, we direct their entire body as well. Look at the ships also, though they are so great and are driven by strong*

winds, are still directed by a very small rudder wherever the inclination of the pilot desires. So also, the tongue is a small part of the body, and yet it boasts of great things.

See how great a small forest is set aflame by such a small fire! And the tongue is a fire, the very world of iniquity; the tongue is set among our members as that which defiles the entire body and sets on fire by hell. For every species of beasts and birds, of reptiles and creatures of the sea, is tamed and has been tamed by the human race. But no one can tame the tongue; it is a restless evil full of deadly poison. With it, we bless our Lord and Father, and with it, we curse men, who have been made in the likeness of God; from the same mouth come both blessing and cursing. My brethren, these things ought not to be this way. Does a fountain send out from the same opening both fresh and bitter water? Can a fig tree, my brethren, produce olives, or a vine produce figs? Nor can salt water produce fresh? (James 3:1–12)

The Overview

James is the half-brother of Jesus, and we learn this story from the books of Mark 6:3 and Matthew 13:55–56. Shortly after Peter leaves Jerusalem to plant new churches, James ascends to prominence as a respectful leader in the Mother Church in Jerusalem, which was made up of primarily Messianic-Christian Jews. This was the first organized Christian community. James was the leader for twenty years, and Christians faced challenging times. A famine led to overwhelming poverty in the region, and Jewish leaders in Jerusalem were heavily oppressing the Messianic Jews. However, James was known and recognized as a pillar in the Jerusalem Church. He was well-known as a peacemaker who fearlessly led with knowledge, wisdom, and godliness until he was tragically martyred. In this book, we see the history of the teachings of James's wisdom, spiritual understanding, and leadership. His teachings have been condensed into a poignant, powerful, and prestigious work.

The book opens like a letter. He greets all the Messianic Jews living outside the Israel region. However, it does not read like Paul's letters, where he addresses specific issues or problems in the local Church. Instead, the book of James is a brief synopsis packed with James's sound wisdom that can be translated, applied, and used in any community of Christians. The teachings can also be applied to Christians today. His objective is not to teach new theological information; instead, he wants to grab the attention of the Christians, present biblical truth from God's perspective, and challenge them to live God's way. In other words, James wants to build a community of mature believers.

This letter is saturated with short wisdom speeches filled with metaphors that make it easy for the student to memorize. In essence, James calls the Messianic community to live their lives drenched with wisdom and, according to Jesus's summary of the Law: to love God and *your neighbor as yourself* (Mark 12:30–31).

The body of the book is in chapters two through five, which consist of twelve short teachings that call and challenge God's people to wholehearted devotion to the way of Jesus Christ. Altogether they don't develop one main idea, but each instruction stands alone and concludes with easy lines to memorize. James's teachings are connected through keywords, phrases, and themes. In the opening body of the book, there are two teachings. First, James addresses favoritism and love. He exposes how we tend to show favor to individuals who can benefit us and ignore and neglect those who cannot. James makes it clear that this behavior is unacceptable and is the opposite of the love that Jesus defines, demonstrates, and displays. Second, James continues to teach and show what genuine faith in Jesus Christ does and does not portray. If an individual says they have faith but neglects and overlooks others who are poor and needy, this individual faith is useless and dead.

James 3:1–12, in the pages of the New Testament, carries incredible and well-sustained teachings on the use, performance, and execution of the

3

tongue. As you read and study the book of James, it's clear he is immersed in the wisdom literature of the Old Testament Scriptures. Much of what James says about the tongue depicts our sinful nature and the failure that contaminates our speech. However, the primary focus of James's teaching is to build mature Christians. So he begins by bringing their attention to those God has called to teach His people.

THE EAGERNESS TO TEACH IN THE CHURCH

James delivers a valuable word of wise counsel to those who aspire to be teachers in God's church.

> *"Let not many of you become teachers, my brethren, knowing that as such we will incur a stricter judgment." (James 3:1)*

Why does James mention teaching, and what does this have to do with the tongue? First, it's crucial that teachers carefully examine the weightiness and potential of their choice of words because words lie at the core and heart of the teaching ministry. An uncontrollable, unreliable, and unruly tongue demonstrate a destructive representation for those learning. James is not writing this as one who has graduated from the school of perfection or has *"arrived."* Instead, he acknowledges his imperfections, inconsistencies, and inadequacies.

> *"For **we** all stumble in many ways." (James 3:1)*

Is it possible James reflected on the days when he *"spoke harshly about Jesus, demeaning His ministry"* (Mark 3:21)? Or was it because Jesus visited him after the resurrection? (1 Cor. 15:7)

James does not exclude himself from this dysfunction (*"For we all"*). We've all spoken words that were ungodly and unkind. One of the keys to spiritual maturity is *"perfecting the tongue"* or *"mastering the tongue."* Either way, the teacher must examine what words we use. So as we explore and examine what James has to say regarding the tongue, we will discover that how we use our tongue is a clear indication and evidence of the location of our spirituality.

Before we go any further, I must ask the question. *"What is the role of a teacher, or what does it mean to teach?"*

WHAT DOES THE BIBLE SAY ABOUT TEACHING?

Teaching is an integral and vital part of everyday life. We make our entrance into this world ignorant. We must learn the necessary lessons and principles so that we're able to manage and maintain life as God would have us: *language proficiency, social skills, moral values, cultural differences, home standards, manners*—all these and so much more are the by-product of the learning process that begins at childhood. God recognizes that teaching is key to obtaining accurate information to help cultivate knowledge. The Bible is a tool to bring understanding to the teaching ministry and its students.

1. Teaching is a gift of the Holy Spirit

> *"Having then gifts differing according to the grace that is given to us, let us use them: if prophecy, let us prophesy in proportion to our faith; or ministry, let us use it in our ministering; he who teaches, in teaching." (Rom. 12:6–8)*

In this Scripture, Paul explains that teaching refers to the God-given ability to explain the Word of God thoroughly. The teacher has been supernaturally endowed to precisely and accurately instruct and communicate understanding and truths of God's Word.

> *"Now you are the body of Christ and members individually. And God has appointed these in the church: first apostles, second prophets, third teachers, after that miracle, then gifts of healings, helps, administrations, varieties of tongues. Are all*

apostles? Are all prophets? Are all teachers? Are all workers of miracles?" (1 Cor. 12:27–29)

Paul asked the question, *"Are all teachers?"* The answer would be an emphatic no! The Body of Christ is broad and filled with every gift imaginable. So likewise, every believer has a gift designated for building, perfecting, and maturing to do effective ministry to advance the Kingdom of God.

For those who God has called to teach in the church, it is a serious assignment because your responsibility is far more significant to the extent of receiving a stricter judgment. It's easy to become complacent and take the calling of teaching as *"trivial"* without considering the cost of responsibility and accountability. Jesus gives us a warning in Luke 12:48:

> *"For everyone to whom much is given, from him much will be required; and to whom much has been committed, of him, they will ask the more."*

Teaching believers is much more than possessing natural and spiritual gifts. There has to be a deeper dimension of a standard of righteous living. James discovered that this area of ministry had become overwhelmingly popular. This was the reason for his admonishing its seriousness. We can't be in such a rush to teach and ignore the accountability and responsibility that falls on the shoulders of the teacher.

> *"Don't be in any rush to become a teacher, my friends. Teaching is highly responsible work. Teachers are held to the strictest standards." (James 3:1)*

2. TEACHING IS A REQUIREMENT AND RESPONSIBILITY FOR ALL PASTORS

1 Timothy 3:2 and 2 Timothy 2:24 tell us that the pastor should have specific qualifications, and one of those qualifications is the ministry of teaching.

*"An overseer, then, must be above reproach, the husband of one
wife, temperate, prudent, respectable, hospitable, able to teach."*

*"The Lord's bond-servant must not be quarrelsome, but be kind
to all, able to teach, patient when wronged."*

The Word of God mandates the pastor to have the ability to teach
sound doctrine consistent with the written Word of God.

"Prescribe and teach these things." (1 Tim. 4:11)

The responsibility of those learning has the mandate to continue the
process of dispersing the Word of God. 2 Timothy 2:2 declares these
words:

*"The things which you have heard from me in the presence of
many witnesses, entrust these to faithful men who will be able
to teach others also."*

SIX PRINCIPLES FOR EFFECTIVE TEACHING IN THE CHURCH

1. The Holy Spirit is your guide
The teacher often attempts to carry the load of conveying God's Word in
their strength. But they should allow the Holy Spirit to guide them to
stay on course.

2. The goal of teaching is to transform lives
In some cases, teachers are responsible for obtaining information to be
transferred rather than getting information to develop life transforma-
tions. Therefore, when preparing a lesson outline, the teacher should avoid
approaching the material with the objective of *"What do I want to teach the
student?"* Instead, the aim should always be *"What do I want the student to
learn and apply?"* Remember, the teacher is the *"tour guide."*

3. Effective teaching engages the student

The student can be an indispensable asset to the lesson. The student should ask questions regarding the dialogue, which can spark a more profound desire for other students to explore their understanding of life issues.

4. An effective teacher is an ongoing learning student

An effective teacher is always searching for innovative ways of staying current and relevant. This requires the teacher's willingness to grow, mature, and stretch their capacity for learning for the student's growth.

5. Effective teachers know their material

One would think this principle is obvious. Unfortunately, in some cases, it is not! I have found that some teachers are glued to their notes, causing them to delay and hinder their ability to teach spontaneously and freely. So that the teacher can feel comfortable teaching freely, they must be in tune with the lesson's content. When the teacher is satisfied with the lesson, they can move freely in the space to interact with the students instead of being attached to the notes.

6. Effective teaching is biblically inspired and driven

The Word of God has to be the force, foundation, and finality to determine the lesson's content. No matter the lessons, Scripture should support and substantiate them. The teaching posture should not be abusive to force personal opinions, ideas, or logic or used as a platform for personal agendas. The teaching must be God's infallible Word.

Chapter Two

DISPROPORTIONATE

"A bit in the mouth of a horse controls the whole horse. A small rudder on a huge ship in the hands of a skilled captain sets a course in the face of the strongest winds. A word out of your mouth may seem of no account, but it can accomplish nearly anything—or destroy it!" (James 3:3–5)

Disproportionate – too large or too small compared to something else.

As I write this book, our nation is in chaos, conflict, and confusion. The coronavirus (COVID-19) has stained this nation and torn the fiber of this country as it experiences a health crisis at an unprecedented level. People all over the country are struggling to try and understand the effects and medical vernacular to manage and maintain the safety guidelines set forth by the Centers for Disease Control. Medical professionals are scrambling and laboring tirelessly to keep the nation informed as the virus wreaks in the country, states, cities, communities, homes, families, lives, churches, and the economy.

Racism has a long, complicated, and controversial history in this country. Unfortunately, the American poison has once again raised its hideous head to an all-time high degree of anger, aggression, hatred, and malice. This evil spirit has caused an even greater divide among people of every ethnicity, generation, and culture. There are protests, rioting, looting, killings, vandalizing, robbing, fighting, and disrespect of every kind filling the streets, highways, and neighborhoods. The coronavirus and racism are spreading like wildfire, destroying lives at an alarming rate. Yet another virus spreads uncontrollably, causing damage along its path, known as *"the tongue."*

When God created the universe, He spoke words, and what He spoke appeared. He *said, "Let there be light,"* and there was light. God *said, "The light was good."* God said, *"Let the waters below the heavens be gathered into one place and let the dry land appear,"* and it was so. Adam was given the authority from the Father to *name* the animals. His authority was accomplished through the power of *"words."* God brilliantly changes Abram's and Jacob's names to reflect their *"new things."* This process came about by using *"words."* Matthew 17:20 tells us, *"If we have faith the size of a mustard seed, you will say to this mountain."* This move of faith involved the use of *"words."* Peter betrayed Jesus three times, the Pharisees conspired to kill Jesus, and Judas sold Jesus for thirty pieces of silver. These three incidents involved *"words."* Words have power! Words have meaning! James, the author, looks closer at our words' use, results, and application.

THE MASTER SWITCH

Several years ago, I purchased a condo, and the HOA (homeowners association) decided to upgrade the wiring. Unfortunately, the electricians caused an interruption to the mainline, which caused the circuit breaker to shut down. The lead electrician entered my condo and proceeded to take a look at my circuit breaker. *"Sir, it looks like you have two lugs that have burned out. They're drawing power from the main utility source after they run through your meter. These lugs are extremely hot, so please be careful. They feed the main panel, distributing it to the smaller breakers. You can flip this lever when you need to shut off the power in the kitchen. This lever is the master switch. When you flip this one, everything turns off."* What he said next was profound. *"I wish my supervisor had a master switch."*

We could all benefit from having one!

James 3:3–5 challenges us to "examine *our tongue.*" When I make an appointment for my annual physical, one of the first exams my primary physician conducts is to have me stick out my tongue. During one visit, I asked her, "*Why do you have me stick out my tongue?*" She explained, "*The tongue indicates signs of illness, coupled with other health issues that may be dormant in the body. It can also help me to determine and offer a precise diagnosis.*" James's examination *challenges* our faith, *tests* our faith, and *displays* our faith. God will use the examination to expose our faith's validity, integrity, and maturity because a "*transformed heart produces a transformed tongue.*" This revelation should prompt every Christian to examine what's spoken from their lips.

The tongue resembles the lugs connected to the circuit breaker. *It's sweltering!* It has an unceasing reserve and storage of sin and can spin out of control. When the tongue spews its venom, the body readily follows, responds, and reacts. We cannot deny its power and destruction. James gives us insight into the power of this organ by spotlighting two explanations that hit us where it hurts.

> "Now if we put the bits into the horses' mouths so that they will obey us, we direct their entire body as well. ⁴ Look at the ships also, though they are so great and are driven by strong winds, are still directed by a very small rudder wherever the inclination of the pilot desires. ⁵ So also the tongue is a small part of the body, and yet it boasts of great things." (James 3:3–5a)

THE BIT

The bit is a piece of metal or synthetic material that fits between the horse's incisors and molars, where there are no teeth, and aids in the communication between the rider and the horse. The bit is part of the harness, which allows the rider to connect with the horse via the reins.

The massiveness and power of a horse can be recognized by all who have sight. I was selected to attend a summer camp for boys at the age of twelve. One of the many activities offered was horseback riding. This is my first time seeing a magnificent creature. Because of their sizeable physique, I revered this large animal and aggressively kept my distance. I could not imagine a 100-pound preteen holding two leather straps as an exact match for the power of a 2,200-pound creature. It's from this perspective James invites our imaginations.

> *"Now if we put the bits into the horses' mouths so that they will obey us, we direct their entire body as well." (James 3:3)*

James makes the opening of this verse straightforward. The bit is small, and when placed in the mouth, it controls the horse's strength. Likewise, the small rudder can turn and guide a large ship. Now James turns the corner. If we have control over our tongue, it indicates that we can control ourselves. Whoever can hold their tongue can bridle (restrain, curb, rein) the whole body. James's point is that the tongue is *disproportionate* to the rest of the body. His point is more specific. The rest of the body is controlled by controlling, checking, and correcting the tongue. If we cannot control, check, and correct the tongue, everything will manifest into chaos, confusion, and catastrophe.

So it's not just difficult to control our speech; when we do the work, we can discipline our whole mind, body, and soul. When we control what we say, we can control how we see everything. We can see life from God's lens. We can see who God wants us to be. We can see where God wants us to go and what He wants us to do in advancing His kingdom. After all, our thoughts are just *"unarticulated"* words. James's point is this: If we want to live in a God-fearing manner, we must master the beauty of speaking in a God-honoring way.

THE BRIDLE/HARNESS

The bit, bridle, and reins function together to give control of the horse's head to the rider. Finally, the harness is the most fundamental part of the horse's headgear. Its function is to direct a horse.

In chapter three, verse three, James paints a startling illustration.

"A bit in the mouth of a horse controls the whole horse."

How in the heavens can something so small control something so massive? Both the horse and the bit are *"disproportionate."* The horse is too large in comparison to the small bit. The animal outweighs the bit, yet the bit controls the horse. When James speaks to us regarding the Christian tongue, he desires us to think about *"control."* A *small* bit in the mouth of an extensive animal controls, maneuvers, directs, and guides its entire body. A small tongue in the mouth of a human being controls and directs the whole body. Who holds the *bit* and *bridle* of your *tongue?* Who controls your words?

Let's take a look at some measurements:

The human tongue
    Average length – 10 cm
    Adult male – 70 grams/3.3 in./8.5 cm
    Adult female – 69 grams/3.1 in./7.9 cm

The bit
    Average length – 5 inches
    Weighs 1–2 pounds

The horse
    Average weight – 900 to 2,200 pounds

There are two points I would like to bring to our attention. First, the weight and size of the tongue do not dismiss, diminish, or disregard its significance and importance. The horse is a large animal, yet the bit is small. It controls movement and direction and "obeys the animal's *rider.*" If I'm controlling a horse and want the animal to perform a specific command or action, the reins put enough pressure on the bit to respond. In other words, the large animal is under the control of the small bit in its mouth. Let's link this same analogy to our tongue. If I'm controlling my tongue and I want my words to perform a specific command or action, then the Holy Spirit acts as the bridle to put enough pressure on my tongue to create and construct my words. When the Holy Spirit holds the bridle, our tongue will not spew poison into the lives of others. It will not speak words of death and destruction. It will not cause others to feel inferior or less valuable. Second, James says, "*The tongue cannot be tamed.*" In other words, on its own, the tongue cannot break from ungodly habits of speech. The writer seems to have a bleak perspective on the tongue and our ability to get this *restless evil* under control.

THE RUDDER

An underwater blade positioned at the stern of a boat or ship and controlled by its helm. Turning causes the vessel's head to turn in the same direction.

The rudder is introduced in the same essence. Instead of a one-pound bit, it is a small rudder. In other words, "In addition to the bit, I want to take a look at the rudder of the ship as well" (James 3:3). He doesn't identify any details regarding the kind of ship. He wants us to use our imagination. James only gives enough information for us to envision large ships. His lack of details might suggest that the size of the vessel is just as big as our creativity and imagination.

A rudder's size can vary depending on the type of ship. Instruments today are more complex due to the advancement of modern technology. For example, cruise ships have GPS devices. This device can hold cruise ships, yachts, and even small fishing boats in place and tell them where they are and their destination. A GPS on a cruise ship is about the size of a laptop computer. This device can be as small as the size of a postage stamp. Imagine something as small as a *postage stamp* can control a cruise ship weighing up to 225,000 (gross tonnage).

Like the bit and the rudder, our tongue is small compared to the horse and the ship. Yet the bit and rudder in the hands of a "*skillful person*" can control the horse and the ship, whereas our bodies cannot control our tongues. This is undoubtedly *"disproportionate."* James states that it seems hopeless for us to control our tongues.

> *"For every species of beasts and birds, of reptiles and creatures of the sea, is tamed as has been tamed by the human race. But no one can tame the tongue; it is a restless evil and full of deadly poison." (James 3:7–8)*

Why Is It So Difficult to Tame the Tongue?

So that we understand what James is saying, we must examine one word in particular. That word is *tame*.

> **Tame** – to make less powerful and easier to control; to cultivate restraint and resistance; to become less dangerous or threatening.

James has a lengthy dialogue regarding the tongue and its decorative and dooming qualities. We've established earlier that the tongue is a small body part, revealing some negative character traits.

+ It is a small part of the body, but it makes a *great boast* (James 3:5)
+ It is a fire and a world of evil that *defiles the whole body* (James 3:6)
+ It is set on *fire by hell* (James 3: 6)
+ It is a *restless evil* and full of *deadly poison* (James 3: 8)

Is it any wonder James declares that taming the tongue is almost impossible?

When Adam and Eve sinned in the Garden of Eden, God assigned and credited sin to all humanity. Whether we want to believe it, all humanity is born with evil and sinful nature (Rom. 3:10–18). Crouching beneath our layers of flesh are varying degrees of pride, jealousy, greed, hatred, bigotry, lust, anger, and bitterness. Satan is in the vicinity when the tongue gets out of control and lashes out. We experience this behavior daily among our families, coworkers, friends, and church.

I've heard the saying, "*Whatever comes up, comes out.*" Oh, how reckless! This character flaw displays a person's level of *"spiritual maturity."* Speech such as this indicates the person has no hands on the reins or rudder; therefore, they say whatever comes into their mind. Then some have conducted their tongue based on their emotions, mindset, and circumstances.

So that we govern our tongue appropriately, James gives us the model to keep the tongue from slipping and sliding toward destroying lives. He points us toward the Holy Spirit, working and developing through the new man, steadily maneuvering His hands on the reins and rudder.

> "*Therefore, if any man be in Christ, he is a new creature, the old (tongue) things passed away; behold new (tongue) have come.*" (2 Cor. 5:17)

Chapter Three

AFLAME

*"Even so, the tongue is a little member and boasts great things.
See how great a forest a little fire kindles! And the tongue is a
fire, a world of iniquity. The tongue is so set among our members that it defiles the whole body and sets on fire the course of
nature, and it is set on fire by hell itself." (James 3:5–6)*

As James gives us another view of the tongue, he challenges our imagination and compares our tongue to fire. What an astounding comparison. So that we truly understand and appreciate this metaphor in its
proper context, we must revisit James 3:5.

*"So also the tongue is a small part of the body, and yet it boasts
of great things. See how great a forest is set aflame by such a
small fire. And the tongue is a fire, the very world of iniquity;
the tongue is set among our members as that which defiles the
entire body, and sets on fire the course of our life, and is set on
fire by hell."*

We must recognize that James repeats the word *tongue* three times in
these two verses and four times in the twelve verses. The fact that James
was repetitive with the word indicates that he wants us to remember
what he's addressing. We can revisit the Old Testament and discover the

many times God repeated Himself. He repeated Himself because He was reminding us of something significant. In John 14:26, Jesus said the Holy Spirit would bring back to our remembrance all things. So when God speaks and repeats certain words or phrases, He wants us to keep what He told us in our thoughts, mind, and memory.

Fire is one of God's unique classical elements known to mankind. With fire and its many benefits, we have access to cooking, burning wood for furnaces and wood-burning ovens, heating our homes, candles to give light to darkness, and fire to destroy garbage. So likewise, the tongue has allowed us to communicate, exhibit, and express affection, taste and praise our Savior and Lord, Jesus Christ. A person with their language under control can speak life and truth into a world where the consensus is to *"say whatever I want to say"* without regard for their words' consequences. However, like unrestrained fire, our tongue can cause significant damage, devastation, and even death. Words do hurt!

Children are told, *"Sticks and stones may break my bones, but words can never hurt me."* As cute as it may sound, this child's rhyme is far from the truth. It's not true, period! The stinging, stabbing, and shooting pain of a tongue spoken against someone can cause grave damage and hurt for a lifetime, many years after the broken bone is healed. Most often, time does not heal wounds. Only when our tongue has been renewed can the wound heal. The Bible gives us many Scriptures to show what happens when we use words constructively and destructively.

+ "A gentle answer turns away wrath, but hard words stir up anger" (Prov. 15:1).
+ "Gentle words bring life and health; a deceitful tongue crushes the spirit" (Prov. 15:4).
+ "A person's words can be life-giving water; words of true wisdom are as refreshing as a bubbling brook" (Prov. 18:4).
+ "Kind words are like honey, sweet to the soul, and healthy for the body" (Prov. 16:24).

"The Tongue Can Either Control or Destroy"

In the introduction, I mentioned the slogan, *"Only you can prevent a forest fire."* And in chapter two, we discovered that small objects control the horse and ship. In this illustration, fire can cause a forest to erupt into ashes due to a tiny flicker from a spark. Likewise, the tongue has the power to cause destruction!

What Is a Spark?

A hot, glowing particle struck from a larger mass; something that sets off a sudden force.

Don't Play with Matches

On this day, my parents were working, and my older siblings cared for the younger ones. I was always the rambunctious, adventurous child who explored, examined, and executed my fascinations. One thing that piqued my curiosity was the flickering of *fire!* When my parents would smoke cigarettes, my father would allow me to strike the match to ignite them. This was the highlight of my day. Because I spent so much time playing alone, I would sneak a book of matches from the kitchen drawer, rush out to play, and not just play. I would find myself setting fire to small objects, such as paper, tree branches, wood, and other things I could get my hands on.

While my parents were watching television and my siblings were outdoors, I decided to crawl under my parents' bed and fire up a cigarette. I was curious to the point of wondering what it was like to smoke a cigarette. But I didn't have matches, I had my father's lighter. I wasn't aware there was a dial on the lighter you could adjust to the level of the flame you desired. If the dial turned to a high level, you could burn yourself. That's what happened. I did not turn the dial to the proper level of flame, and I burned my upper lip. I screamed, and my parents found me under the bed in tears from the pain. From that experience, my parents taught me never to play with any devices that produce fire, and my father ensured that never happened again!

This incident could've been disastrous for my family and me. The tiny flame could have spiraled out of control because of my negligence. Our tongue can cause the same damage if it is not contained and controlled!

Another person's choice of words to me, and my choice of words to them, can last for quite some time, whether for good or evil. An insensitive remark can inflict lasting injury on others. On the other hand, responding promptly with words of encouragement can change a person's life course. Proverbs 16:24 declares this:

> "Kind words are like honey, sweet to the soul, and healthy for the body."

Let's examine this passage of Scripture more closely. The first two words, "Kind words," set the tone for this verse. Our choice of words can turn a situation into *honey* or *hatred*. They can be *sweet to the soul* or *sour to the soul*. Our words can bring *healing* (*heal-thy*) to the body or *harm*.

"Words Can Hurt, and Words Can Heal!"

Proverbs speaks of someone who does not consider their words' destructive, devastating power.

> "Like a madman who throws firebrands, arrows, and death, is the man who deceives his neighbor, and says, 'I was only joking.'" (Prov. 26:18–19).

What are firebrands? Firebrands are instigators, inciters, or provokers who lead illicit activities. They deliberately initiate trouble, mischief, and confusion.

When we think about the behavior of someone's anger, in this case, Solomon describes the person as being a "*madman.*" This person has lost control of their anger; they deliberately spew words of destruction.

Solomon says their words are provoking, sharp as arrows, and strong enough to cause death.

James is not saying we should never speak or commit to silence. But, of course, it would be easier than exercising self-control over our vicious tongues. In our previous chapters, we've learned that the bridle, rudder, and fire can all do enormous good when controlled, constrained, and corrected.

"THE TONGUE CORRUPTS MAN'S TOTAL BEING"

Proverbs 26:18–19 gives a great illustration of this. Please allow me to translate this verse into modern-day vernacular.

"A man who deceives and disguises his deception and uses it as a joke is as dangerous as a lunatic shooting poisonous arrows in a crowd." Someone may become injured and or could die. Lying is never to be taken lightly, especially in a joking manner. Often the effects of the arrow may not appear immediately. However, the sting may take days and sometimes weeks. We must remember that lying is a *"sin,"* bringing death. His actions may have serious consequences, though it may not be his intent. It's never an excuse to say, *"I didn't mean any harm!"*

The firebrand and arrow represent the power and destruction of our tongue. The provoking language coupled with the poisonous arrow is a deadly combination because the tongue can *"corrupt our total being."* An uncontrolled, unruly, and unrestrained tongue can kill mentally, spiritually, and in some cases, physically. Once the words are released from our lips, we cannot retrieve them. The damage is done! The arrow is discharged, and our words have caused another person discomfort. How tragic!

> *"When there are many words, transgression is unavoidable.*
> *But he who restrains his lips is wise. The tongue of the righ-*
> *teous is as choice silver, The heart of the wicked is worth little.*
> *The lips of the righteous feed many, But fools die for lack of*
> *understanding." (Prov. 10:19–21)*

There aren't many sins where the tongue is not in the vicinity and engaged in the conversation. The fewer words, the less the possibility of the presence of sin. Sins of the tongue originated in our sinful nature. In Proverbs 6:16–19, Solomon shows us that out of the seven sins that God despises, three of them involve the use of the tongue:

> "There are six things which the LORD hates, Yes, seven which are an abomination to Him: Haughty eyes, a lying tongue, And hands that shed innocent blood, A heart that devises wicked plans, Feet that run rapidly to evil, A false witness who utters lies, And one who spreads strife among brothers."
> "Come, you children, listen to me; I will teach you the fear of the LORD. Who is the man who desires life and loves the length of days that he may see good? Keep your tongue from evil and your lips from speaking deceit. Depart from evil and do good; Seek peace and pursue it." (Ps. 34:11–14)

Sins of the tongue are influenced by our sinful nature and produce sins such as bitterness, greed, arrogance, discord, jealousy, sexual immorality, perversion, hatred, strife, adultery, etc. Every Christian has experienced one or more of these areas at some stage of their spiritual sojourn. For example, when someone verbally attacks another person, the tongue is positioned and ready to voice the condition of their heart. Jesus echoes these words in Matthew 12:34:

> "You brood of vipers, how can you, being evil, speak what is good? For the mouth speaks out of that which fills the heart."

And in Genesis 4:7, God tells Cain, "If you do what is right, will you not be accepted? But if you refuse to do what is right, sin is crouching at your door. It desires to have you, but you must rule over it."

"It Is Our Responsibility to Rule over Our Tongue"

"God blessed them; and God said to them, "Be fruitful and multiply, and fill the earth, and subdue it; and rule over the fish of the sea and over the birds of the sky and over every living thing that moves on the earth." (Gen. 1:28)

When God gave man their assignment, He gave them His identity and rulership. He said, *"Subdue [rule, have dominion over] the earth!"* Do you realize how much authority He has given us? Let's examine the word *subdue*.

Subdue – to bring a nation, country, or people under control by force; to control, rule, or have dominion over.

God gave us the authority to rule, control, and dominate the earth. So likewise, our words have the power to take control of the world as God created it. One of the many ways we can accomplish this is through the power of our tongue.

If we want to show the condition of our hearts, we don't have to search very far. It's directly in front of us. Our tongues will always reveal what's in our hearts. What if you knew something wrong about someone or suspected something was out of the ordinary? Would you share this information with others or talk to the person privately to discuss the matter? If in doubt, don't discuss it with anyone! The moment you share with someone other than the guilty party, it becomes *"gossip,"* which leads to malicious behavior. So Paul tells us in Ephesians 4:29:

"Let no unwholesome word proceed from your mouth, but only such a word as is good for edification according to the need of the moment, so that it will give grace to those who hear."

GOSSIP: CONSTRUCTOR OR DESTRUCTOR

The Hebrew word "gossip" is *"one who discloses secrets or scandals."* A gossiper is a person who has privileged information regarding another person. Gossipers' ultimate goal is to elevate themselves by tearing down others—exalting themselves as the chief commanding officer of knowledge. Gossipers focuses on the failings, faults, and frailty of others and discloses possibly damaging, embarrassing, shameful, and condemning personal details regarding the lives of others.

As Christians, we must guard our tongues, lips, and mouths and do all we can to refrain from the sinful act of gossip. However, if we surrender our desires, wants, and needs to the Lord Jesus Christ, then and only then will He help us remain vigilant and righteous in our efforts to please Him in our speech.

> *"May the words of my mouth and the meditation of my heart, be acceptable in thy sight, O Lord my strength and my Redeemer."*
> (Ps. 19:14)

Chapter Four

A WANTON KILLER

"For every species of beasts and birds, of reptiles and creatures of the sea, is tamed and has been tamed by the human race. But no one can tame the tongue; it is a restless evil and full of deadly poison. With it, we bless our Lord and Father, and with it, we curse men, who have been made in the likeness of God." (James 3:7–9)

In chapters one and two, we see that the bridle and rudder can control a large animal and a large ship, and yet God declares through the Apostle James, *"No man can tame the tongue."* I appreciate how the Message Bible translates James 3:7–9:

"This is scary: You can tame a tiger, but you can't tame a tongue—it's never been done. The tongue runs wild, a wanton killer. With our tongues, we bless God our Father; with the same tongues, we curse the very men and women he made in His image. Curses and blessings out of the same mouth!"

"But You Can't Tame the Tongue—It's Never Been Done!"

It is scary to think that we cannot tame our *"dental danger—the tongue."* Countless times I've asked, *"Can I tame my tongue?"* The answer always returns, "*No!*" Although words out of our mouths may seem of no regard, they can accomplish, achieve, and attain primarily anything and destroy and devastate everything.

As we study Scripture, we see that David was a man after God's own heart (1 Sam. 13:14, Acts 13:22); unlike most of us, he prayed about his words. For example, in Psalm 19:14, David prays this prayer:

> "*Let the words of my mouth and the meditation of my heart be acceptable in Your sight, O Lord, my rock and my redeemer.*"

Let's examine David's prayer of surrender using the power of his words. The first six words give precedence and insight into the posture of his heart. But, first, David focused on what he said. He wasn't concerned with restraining the tongue because he knew that when his words aligned with his heart, the tongue would follow.

Unlike King David, most of us are unaware and do not pray about what we speak—only the restraining and detaining of our tongue. David makes it clear that his ultimate goal was to be sure that the purity and posture of his heart was acceptable and pleasing to God. Nothing else mattered!

In our highly technological culture, where complacency has become a normality in poor speech, one might seem overwhelming in consciously choosing not to sin with their mouth. "*Impossible,*" one might respond. Yet, it is attainable and achievable when we trust and rely on the Lord Jesus Christ for strength to help us perform, perfect, and produce fruit in our lives.

So that we understand the importance of taming the tongue, we must first examine and explore the "*right and wrong use of the tongue.*" Throughout James's letter, he has much to say about this matter that might suggest the church was guilty of committing what he calls "*sins of the tongue.*"

> "*Come, you children, listen to me; I will teach you the fear of the Lord. Who is the man who desires life and loves the length of days that he may see good? Keep your tongue from evil and*

your lips from speaking deceit. Depart from evil and do good;
Seek peace and pursue it." (Ps. 34:11–14)

So James very candidly teaches us that the tongue of a Christian is the gauge that discloses the believer's spiritual growth and maturity. Our words reveal what kind of Christians we are and the condition of our hearts. So that we have a greater understanding, James uses three illustrations to demonstrate the effectiveness and power of *"dental danger— the tongue."*

1. Our tongue has the power to direct
2. Our tongue can destroy
3. Our tongue has the power to delight

1. Our tongue has the power to direct

James 3:3-4 brilliantly paints the imagery of the horse's bit and the ship's rudder. Whether we want to believe it, our words can *"direct or steer"* others into the right or wrong path. For example, if I were to ask you how to get to I-90/94 East, and you proceed to give me directions for I-290 West, you have given me the wrong directions. Therefore, I will end up someplace I never intended, and it could cause delays, drama, and possibly disaster. What do I mean? Going in the direction of I-290 could be all sorts of detours. The wrong directions have caused discomfort. Proverbs 18:21 tells us,

> *"Death and life are in the power of the tongue, And those who*
> *love it will eat its fruit."*

God wants us to be aware of a shiftless word, the half-truth, the talkative storyteller, and the decorative liar. All these players can change one's life drastically and lead it down a path of destruction. But, on the other hand, speech seasoned with honey can direct a person out of sinful behavior and onto salvation!

2. Our tongue can destroy

James's depiction in chapters three, five, through eight highlights the size of the tongue. Though it is small, it possesses a heavy delivery of destruction. Let's take a look at Matthew 12:34–35:

> "You brood of vipers, how can you, being evil, speak what is good? For the mouth speaks out of that which fills the heart. The good man brings out of his good treasure what is good, and the evil man brings out of his evil treasure what is evil."

Let's continue looking into what James says about the devastation and effects of the tongue. "A tiny spark can set a whole forest on fire, and the tongue is like a small flame (James 3:5)." In this illustration, he uses a "spark" as the culprit. The spark represents the tongue. This lets us know that the tongue can cause severe damage to destroy everything in its path. King Solomon confirms James's illustration.

> "A worthless man digs up evil. While his words are like scorching fire." (Prov. 16:27)

If an evil tongue can spread poison, imagine what would happen if the tongue spread love, peace, joy, kindness, patience, goodness, faithfulness, and self-control? However, a Christian's language is like "medicine"; it will heal and not hurt. It will cure and not curse. It will build and not bruise. It will repair and not rupture. It will restore and not ruin. It will reconcile and not refuse.

> "Truthful lips will be established forever. But a lying tongue is only for a moment." (Prov. 12:19)

3. Our tongue has the power to delight

What if I gave you some apple seeds to plant an apple orchard? You plant the seeds, and one year later, you go and check to see how the trees are progressing. To your amazement, you don't see apples; you see lemons. This is not what you planted. You want to see what was produced—apples! What appeared on the trees is not what you planted. The seed has contradicted itself. You want to see healthy, ripe, juicy apples!

James 3:9–12, the writer points out the impossibility of such a contradiction. If bad fruit and bitter water continue to come from the same spring, it signifies no contradiction. In other words, the tree and the spring are both terrible. If I planted rotten apples, I should not expect ripe ones.

It would be a travesty to see a fig tree grow olive berries or olive berries grow fig trees. It would be just as unnatural for a Christian to continue living in sin when we're supposed to be the salt of the earth. In the same manner, the tongue cannot speak blessing and cursing, and a tree cannot bear two kinds of fruit (Prov. 18:4 and 18:20–21).

> *"Unless you are regenerated, born from above by a new and heavenly birth, you are not Christians, whatever you may be called, and you cannot produce the fruit which is acceptable to God any more than a fig tree can produce olive berries."*
> —Charles Spurgeon

How Can We Control Our Mouths?
1. Take notice and beware of "pitfalls" —James 3:2

+ News Flash: *"We all stumble with our mouths!"* There are several ways this can happen.
+ Lying (Eph. 4:25)
+ Boasting (Prov. 27:2)
+ Cursing (Rom. 12:14)
+ Complaining (Phil. 2:14)
+ Being Critical of others (Eph. 4:29)
+ Not following through (James 5:12—The Message)
+ Outburst of anger (Gal. 5:20)
+ Social Media (Facebook, Twitter, Instagram, TikTok, Linkedin, Snapchat, Pinterest, Reddit)

+ Sexting

2. Be deliberate and speak with confidence, self-worth, and self-assurance

+ What you say to others can make an enormous *"impact"* on their lives. —James 3:3
+ Complimenting others
+ Constructive criticism
+ Helping others
+ Building others
+ Inspiring others
+ Adding worth and value to others
+ Encouraging others
+ Befriending others

3. Be careful, and think before you speak

+ Our words can potentially escalate or alleviate a situation because of our speech. —James 3:5
+ *Think before you speak!* It starts with being quiet, listening, comprehending, and interacting. It all takes place before opening our mouths. Our responsibility is to check and control our tongue.

4. Be graceful and gentle in our execution

If your words are not gentle and graceful, you probably should not be speaking them. —James 3:6. Proverbs 16:1 says, *"A gentle answer turns away wrath, But a harsh word stirs up anger."* Most of us want to enter a situation peacefully. However, sometimes we have a slight memory lapse and forget our spirituality is at stake. Our tone has caused the problem to get out of control because our words are out of control. How we approach others is just as important as the words we choose.

Chapter Five

BUILDING OR BURYING

I recently had a conversation with my nephew when he asked, *"Is it true that life and death are in the power of the tongue?"* And he took it a step further and asked, *"What does my tongue have to do with someone living or dying?"* What powerful questions. They were so powerful they caused me to pause and think. I needed to examine both questions carefully and cautiously. I felt the only sure approach to answering was to refer to God's Word for clarity and understanding. Proverbs 4:7 says this:

> *"Wisdom is the principle thing; therefore, get wisdom, and in all they getting, get understanding."*

Before I take on this enormous task of answering these questions, I must tackle the word *wisdom*. James tells us:

> *"If any of you lacks wisdom, let him ask God, who gives to all generously and without reproach, and it will be given to him."* (James 1:5)

All of life, whether good, bad, ugly, or indifferent, might suggest that we acquire and apply *wisdom*. God granted us this tool to help us make the right decisions in every area of life. Before we embark upon any significant decisions that will affect how we live and the lives of our families, *wisdom* should be the focal point of all decision-making. So what is wisdom?

There is a story in the Bible that speaks of Solomon, a young man to whom God offered anything his heart desired.

> *Now Solomon loved the LORD, walking in the statutes of his father David, except he sacrificed and burned incense on the high places. The king went to Gibeon to sacrifice there, for that was the great high place; Solomon offered a thousand burnt offerings on that altar. In Gibeon, the LORD appeared to Solomon in a dream at night; and God said, "Ask what you wish Me to give you."*

> *Then Solomon said, "You have shown great lovingkindness to Your servant David, my father, according as he walked before You in truth and righteousness and uprightness of heart toward You; and You have reserved for him this great lovingkindness, that You have given him a son to sit on his throne, as it is this day. Now, O LORD my God, You have made Your servant king in place of my father David, yet I am but a little child; I do not know how to go out or come in. Your servant is in the midst of Your people, which You have chosen, a great people who are too many to be numbered or counted. So give Your servant an understanding heart to judge Your people to discern between good and evil. For who is able to judge this great people of Yours?*

> *It was pleasing in the sight of the Lord that Solomon had asked this thing. God said to him, "Because you have asked this thing and have not asked for yourself long life, nor have asked riches for yourself, nor have you asked for the life of your enemies, but have asked for yourself discernment to understand justice, behold, I have done according to your words. Behold, I have*

given you a wise and discerning heart so that there has been no
one like you before you, nor shall one like you arise after you. I
have also given you what you have not asked, both riches and
honor so that there will not be any among the kings like you
all your days. If you walk in My ways, keeping My statutes
and commandments, as your father David walked, then I will
prolong your days." (1 Kings 3:3–14)

According to what you've just read, wisdom is:

"The capacity of the mind that allows us to comprehend, under-
stand and apply God's rule, reign, and righteousness into our
lives from His perspective. Wisdom is simply conducting life
God's way, not ours!"

Now that we have a greater understanding of wisdom let's deal with the
matter. If wisdom is doing life God's way, then our words must be pleasing
to God and according to His Word. Any other way outside of God's will
would be considered a sin. For example, "Is it true that life and death are
in the power of the tongue?"

In the Old and New Testament, the word *"tongue"* is used literally and
metaphorically. First, however, we must remember this word often refer-
ences the *"spoken word."* This *"spoken word"* or *"figure of speech"* is known
as *"metonymy."* This is when one word, thing, or concept is referred to by
the name of something closely associated with an item, word, or idea. An
example of metonymy appears in this phrase. *"The pen is mightier than the*
sword."

+ *"Pen"* stands for *"the written word."*
+ *"Sword"* stands for *"military aggression."*

This means that *"thinking and writing have more influence, impact, and*
importance on people, events, and circumstances than the use of aggression,

anger, force, or violence." In other words, words have more power than weapons. Proverbs 15:4 says it best,

> *"Gentle words are a tree of life; a deceitful tongue crushes the spirit."*

The word *"tongue"* is a metonymy. A literal, uncontrolled tongue cannot crush the human spirit. However, the words the tongue produce can!

> *"When we open the dictionary, it gives us definitions of many words. However, the heart does not give us its condition or definition until we open our mouths."*

The words the tongue produces affect three areas that can shift the course of our lives. Because of its venom, the tongue's sting destroys relationships, marriages, churches, corporations, businesses, etc. Let's take a look at these areas.

EMOTIONAL

Human emotions vary from person to person. Yet they are similar regarding the powerful effect and vulnerability of injury the tongue can cause. James 3:6 defines the tongue as a *"fire."* The primary damage a fire can cause is burning. And who has not been burned by the tongue? Yet, if the tongue can burn, it can also heal. Proverbs 15:4 describes what a healing, kind, and encouraging tongue can accomplish.

> *"Kind words heal and help; cutting words wound and maim."*

I appreciate the Message translation because it gives the reader a vivid view. *"Cutting words wound and maim."* What a description of an untamed tongue's damage to others. To maim someone implies the loss or injury of a body part through a violent act. When our words *"maim"* someone, this is what happens.

It *"cripples"* them *"emotionally."*
It *"mutilates"* them *"emotionally."*
It *"mangles"* them *emotionally*

> *"When we maim others with our words, it deprives them of being effective in every area of their lives. The wound has become emotional, severely deep, and damaged. What we say can have a profound effect on others!"*
>
> –Zachary W. Lavender

PHYSICAL

Words can create a plethora of actions, whether good or bad. A friendly game of playing cards can quickly shift and get the competitive juices going. But when one player feels threatened by another, their words can cause the game to suffer. A judge or jury can cause a person to be killed or to live simply by their words. The Bible tells us love is a word of action. However, what would intimacy, romance, passion, and fascination be without the beauty of words? Vocal music has melody, harmony, rhythm, timbre, and tempo. But what would these elements be without words? The weatherman announces the forecast, a doctor delivers a diagnosis, and the football coach gives the play for the next game. How often have we murdered someone or caused an argument with our words? The truth: the tongue does indeed have power, potential, and propensity to create life or death.

SPIRITUAL

From a medical standpoint, what exams are performed to determine the heart's condition? There are several to detect when there's an interruption in the heart's function. One of these is called an *echocardiogram*. What is an *echocardiogram?*

This exam is a graphic outline of the heart's health, movement, and function. It can detect artery blockages, heart disease, or abnormalities in the heart's walls. God has given us an *"echocardiogram"* called the Holy Spirit to see the health of our hearts. Jeremiah 17:10 and Romans 8:27 says,

"I, the LORD, search the heart, I test the mind, Even to give to each man according to his ways, According to the results of his deeds."

"And He who searches the hearts knows what the mind of the Spirit is because He intercedes for the saints according to the will of God."

All humanity is incapable of taming and controlling the tongue because it is an unruly, restless, uneasy, discontented, an unquiet evil, full of deadly venom. Conversely, a tongue under control marks the Christian's commitment to the Holy Spirit's leading. Aside from accepting Jesus's death on the cross, we will one day be judged according to our words. Matthew 12:37 says,

"For by your words, you will be justified, and by your words, you will be condemned."

Our Father created us as *"spiritually expressive beings."* Therefore, we are never deficient in the area of communication. This is why God gave man the gift of designing audio recordings, Braille for the visually impaired, sign language for the deaf, and many forms of communication.

CHARACTER OF CONTRADICTION

"With it, we bless our Lord and Father, and with it, we curse men, who have been made in the likeness of God; from the same mouth come both blessing and cursing. My brethren, these things ought not to be this way. Does a fountain send out from the same opening both fresh and bitter water? Can a fig tree, my brethren, produce olives, or a vine produce figs? Nor can salt water produce fresh." (James 3:9–12)

What truth and revelation. Just take the time to listen to what others are saying and listen to the things you say. Those with whom we are closely associated—family, friends, coworkers, and conversations passing on the street. We can hear them cursing one minute, professing the name of Jesus Christ, and the next saying things of joy and delight. This kind of speech is a *"contradiction."* What is the meaning of *contradiction*?

> "A combination of words, ideas, situations, phrases, or statements opposed to one another; when two statements don't seem to agree with each other."

It's disturbing to imagine anyone using unkind, evil, abusive, disrespectful words to honor God. Perhaps we were thinking that James may be referring to non-Christians or those who have not accepted Jesus as their Savior and Lord. Or we may imagine he's describing *"other people"*—not Christians. News flash! James is describing you and me—Christians. He's speaking to the ones who have the tongue of worship. He's openly outlining every believer's deficiency, flaw, frailty, and weakness.

Believe it or not, Christians, as well as unbelievers, use words to curse others. In Greek, the words *"curse"* means to condemn another person. Generally, this type of speech is a desire for another person to experience evil.

It has become the norm to curse others without regard for others' feelings. We dismiss it as not *"that big of a deal."* When in fact, it's a serious deal! As James states in verse 9 of chapter three,

"We curse men, who have been made in the likeness of God."

It Doesn't Make Sense

How is it possible to bless God in one breath and then turn around and curse the one created in God's image? It doesn't make sense. How can it be that the tongue can speak good and bad from the same vessel? James asks two questions that make it challenging for a Christian:

1. Does a spring send forth fresh *water* and *bitterness* from the same opening?
2. Can a fig tree, my brethren, bear olives, or grapevine bear figs?

James makes a solid case that humanity is not innately endowed to control its tongue. If that were the case, how would it be possible for the Christian to use words to honor God and curse others to mirror Him? James says, *"This not ought to be so."* It *doesn't make sense!* Using words to curse others is " contradictory and against God's creation." It creates a contradiction and conflict against God's nature. James gives a vivid analogy of a system where water flows out of the earth, creating an aquifer for fresh water. Nowhere in God's creation will you find a combination of saltwater and freshwater streaming up from the ground. Again, *it doesn't make sense.* Fresh water and salt water are two completely different sources. Just as words of blessing and cursing come from two distinct natures—*spirit and flesh,* Christians should not release both blessings and curses from their mouths. The fact that our tongue will sometimes lose control is evidence that we are badly *broken, bruised, battered,* and in need of repair and repentance.

James takes his case further and addresses that the tongue is habitually out of control. To give us a glimpse and taste of contradiction, he penned in the previous verse that a spring of water will never pour out two kinds of water—*it doesn't make sense.* Then he tells us that no fig tree can grow olives, nor can a grapevine produce figs. And would you expect to dip your cup in a pond and pull up fresh water? *It has never been done!*

As I continued studying verses 9–12, I noticed after verse 12, James never mentions the tongue again. He abruptly shifts the subject and gives no explanation or instructions on how we can solve the problem. Instead, James expects us to trust God to help us change our speech choices. We are flawed through and through, far from perfection. However, our tongues will align with God's words as we grow in grace, wisdom, and knowledge. The words of the Father will flow through us!

Chapter Seven

THE TONGUE AND HEART CONNECTION

"For there is no good tree which produces bad fruit, nor, on the other hand, a bad tree which produces good fruit. For each tree is known by its own fruit. For men do not gather figs from thorns, nor do they pick grapes from a briar bush. The good man out of the good treasure of his heart brings forth what is good, and the evil man out of the evil treasure brings forth what is evil; for his mouth speaks from that which fills his heart." (Luke 6:43–45)

"You don't get wormy apples off a healthy tree, nor good apples off a diseased tree. The health of the apple tells the health of the tree. You must begin with your own life-giving lives. It's who you are, not what you say and do, that counts. Your true being brims over into true words and deeds." (Luke 6:43–45)

In these two translations, Jesus tells us how to judge a person's character, integrity, and actions. This can be done much like we view a tree or plant to know if it's a *"good plant"* or not.

"For there is no good tree which produces bad fruit, nor, on the other hand, a bad tree which produces good fruit. For each

tree is known by its own fruit. For men do not gather figs from thorns, nor do they pick grapes from a briar bush." (Luke 6:43–44)

If we want to know what kind of tree or plant we possess, look at the fruit of the individual. For example, a pear tree sounds like a good tree. However, if you have a Bradford pear tree, you will get small, inedible pears. What's on the inside—what the tree produces will determine what kind of fruit it brings forth. Jesus says the same is true about humanity.

From this scripture, people can be judged by their words and actions because they disclose what lurks from within. Listen to their words if you want to know what is brewing inside a person. It's just that simple. We often hear a familiar phrase: *"Don't judge me!"*

A LESSON ON JUDGING

Jesus tells us in Matthew 7:1–2,

> *"Do not judge so that you will not be judged. For in the way you judge, you will be judged; and by your standard of measure, it will be measured to you."*

Jesus is not telling others not to judge us. He's telling us not to judge others. What others do is not our initial concern. Our challenge is not how others judge us *but how we judge them.* When Jesus says, *"Judge not,"* He's not sending mixed messages about judging others. He wants us to take great care of how we judge others. He tells us in Matthew 7:3–5,

> *"Why do you look at the speck that is in your brother's eye, but do not notice the log that is in your own eye? Or how can you say to your brother, 'Let me take the speck out of your eye,' and behold, the log is in your own eye? You hypocrite, first take the log out of your own eye, and then you will see clearly to take the speck out of your brother's eye."*

It would not be wrong to lovingly and carefully help our brother or sister remove a harmful speck from their eye. However, it's wrong to self-righteously point out a speck in their eye when we ignore and dismiss the large bole protruding from ours.

"JUDGE AT YOUR OWN RISK"

According to the Bible, a "distinct connection" joins the heart and tongue. They work together like bread and butter, salt and pepper. Mark 7:21–23 confirms this:

> "For from within, out of the heart of men, proceed the evil thoughts, fornications, thefts, murders, adulteries, deeds of coveting and wickedness, as well as deceit, sensuality, envy, slander, pride, and foolishness. All these evil things proceed from within and defile the man."

These impious sins originate directly from the heart, and then the tongue carries the person onto a path of destruction. Proverbs 14:3 says,

> "In the mouth (words) of the foolish is a rod for his back, But the lips (words) of the wise will protect them."

> "The tongue (words) of the wise makes knowledge acceptable, But the mouth (words) of fools spouts folly." (Prov. 15:2)

THE HEART IS THE DATABASE; THE TONGUE IS THE OUTLET

A computer has four primary functions.

1. Input Function
2. Process Function
3. Output Function
4. Storage Function

1. Input Function
The function of an input device is to communicate information to a computer or other processing equipment. The most common forms of input devices are the keyboard and the mouse.

2. Process Function
Once the input function has received the user's data and instructions, the computer starts the processing function.

3. Output Function
Output devices provide data in different forms. For example, monitors and printers are commonly used devices with a computer.

4. Storage Function
Data storage consists of computer components and recording media to retain digital data.

Just as the computer has four functions, the tongue has four functions.

1. To Measure
2. To Manage
3. To Strengthen
4. To Shield

1. James 3:1–2 "To Measure"
The tongue is our *"measuring tool."* One of its functions is to measure our "maturity." Our faith will never exceed our words!

2. James 3:3–5 "To Manage."
We must *"manage"* what we put in our hearts so that the tongue can speak words that will inevitably keep things on the right path. It will either construct life or destroy life.

3. James 3:6–8 "To Strengthen."
Out of all the body members, the tongue has the power to cause the most damage. This organ is a *"powerful force."* Because of its power, the Word of God tells us it can "extend life" or "end life (Proverbs 18:21)." God did not create the tongue to "kill others." Instead, to create an abundant life that glorifies Him and helps others to grow to spiritual maturity.

4. James 3:9–18 "To Shield."
When we hear the word *"shield,"* we immediately associate it with *guard, protect, defend,* or *cover.* Yet, proverbs 4:23 says, *"Guard your heart above all else, for it determines the course of your life."* James pushes us to shield our hearts so that our words can bring peace into the lives of others. In other words, our tongue either creates love, joy, peace, patience, kindness, goodness, faithfulness, gentleness, and self-control or reveals evil and, eventually, death.

A HEALTHY HEART BREEDS A HEALTHY TONGUE
During my research, I discovered a spiritual connection that aligns the tongue and the heart on the same course. The heart plays the role of the *"storage function,"* and the tongue plays the part of the *"output function."* In other words, the heart is the *"database,"* and the tongue is the *"outlet."* When we want to create a document, we proceed to the computer and type information into a document. When we've completed the document, we press the *"save"* key to *"store"* the information on the computer. When it's time to use the document, we press the *"print"* key, and the document is produced. What we have on the document is the information we typed and stored. The computer will only print what was held in the database onto the document.

When we spend quiet and quality time daily studying the Bible, His Words are stored in our hearts, mind, and soul. Proverbs 7:3 says,

> *"Bind them on your fingers; Write them on the tablet of your heart."*

In the Bible, there are several places where you will find God writing on *"the tablets of our hearts."* We will look at two of them.

> *"You are our letter, written in our hearts, known and read by all men; being manifested that you are a letter of Christ, cared for by us, written not with ink but with the Spirit of the living God, not on tablets of stone but tablets of human hearts."* (2 Cor. 3:2–3)

> *"Do not let kindness and truth leave you; Bind them around your neck, Write them on the tablet of your heart."* (Prov. 3:3)

Christians have been called to be *"letters"* for Jesus Christ. These letters are God's Laws written not just on stone tablets but on *"human tablets,"* the heart. As Christians, we commit and dedicate our lives to living according to the infallible Word of God. We are the light, salt, example, and representation of Christ. Therefore, our words should mimic those of Christ. When we look at His life, His words healed, delivered, made us whole, set us free, gave compassion, loved unselfishly, and so much more.

As followers of Christ, our ultimate goal is to live a life that pleases Him through our conduct, character, and example, not just our *"words."* It starts with the proper nutrition we're feeding the heart. Then, the outlet will reveal what we provide the database—the heart and the tongue.

Chapter Eight

HOW DO WE CONTROL AND TAME THE TONGUE?

"But no man can tame the tongue." (James 3:8)

To live righteous and fruitful lives, we must learn the importance of *"controlling our tongue."* We must try to put restraint, resistance, and restrictions on the words that proceed from our mouths.

Each of us is solely responsible for every word that we speak. Not only are we accountable for our words, but God also holds us accountable.

> *"But I tell you that every careless word that people speak, they shall give an accounting for it in the day of judgment."* (Matt. 12:36)

Perhaps we should look closer to examine the word *tame* or *taming*. Its origin is early Middle Eastern, and its meaning is,

> *"in a state of subjection, physically subdued, restrained in behavior; to constrain, to force, to break from; to tie up, fasten."*

Learning to tame the tongue may not be as easy as one may think. There's a reason James makes a bold statement in saying, *"But no man can* tame the tongue." Because in our human flesh, it's impossible to do without the help of the Holy Spirit. However, when we're in Christ and He's in us, there's nothing we cannot do! The writer confirms this in Phil. 4:13.

> "I can do all things through Christ who strengthens me."

I stated earlier when Adam sinned in the Garden, God attributed Adam's sin to all humanity:

> "Therefore, just as through one man sin entered into the world, and death through sin, and so death spread to all men because all sinned." (Rom. 5:12)

At that very moment, every human being born after Adam would be born with a wicked heart; evil, sinful nature; and a poisonous tongue (Rom. 3:10–18).

Taming the Tongue

So that we tame our tongue, this daily battle requires constant *evaluation, examination,* and *exercise.* We must be vigilant and persistent in not allowing *"dental danger"* to run loose, destroying the lives of others. Essentially our tongue gets grossly inflamed with anger, malice, aggression, resentment, gossip, and the like. The poor use of our words can lead to the tongue causing chaos in our lives and the lives of others. But we cannot do this in our own strength. *We need help!*

> "And the tongue is a fire, the very world of iniquity; the tongue is set among our members as that which defiles the entire body, and sets on fire the course of our life, and is set on fire by hell." (James 3:6)

WHICH ONE WILL YOU FEED?

In the movie *Tomorrowland*, there's an interaction between the father and daughter where the young lady reminds her father of a story he continues to share with her. She's bored with hearing the story and goes on to tell her father, "*There were two wolves who are constantly fighting with each other. One is represented as darkness and despair. The other is light and hope.*" The question I pose to you is: *Which one wins?* You're probably wondering, "*What does this have to do with my words?*"

God has made humanity "*free agents.*" He has given us the freedom to choose our words. A large majority of our words can bring "*darkness and doom,*" and a percentage of our words can bring "*light and life.*" As "*free agents,*" we have words that build, construct, encourage, inspire, and promote spiritual growth. Then we have words that tear down, destroy, demolish, and devour. Finally, we have words that proceed from our mouths, never to be spoken. These verses give us greater insight:

> "*He who guards his mouth and his tongue, Guards his soul from troubles.*" (Prov. 21:23)

> "*Either make the tree good and its fruit good, or make the tree bad and its fruit bad; for the tree is known by its fruit. You brood of vipers, how can you, being evil, speak what is good? For the mouth speaks out of that which fills the heart.*" (Matt. 12:33–34)

Let's revisit James 3:8:

> "*But no one can tame the tongue; it is a restless evil and full of deadly poison.*"

James gives us no help or hope in this area. And he does not provide us with a solid fix for this problem. If we can't tame our tongue, what's the point in trying? I have discovered that the only sure way to tame our tongue is by collaborating and working with the Holy Spirit. This problem cannot be resolved or refined by mere self-power. Matthew says,

> *"And looking at them Jesus said to them, 'With people this is impossible, but with God all things are possible." (Matt. 19:26)*

If we want to win this battle of the *"untamed tongue,"* we must starve the *"wolf of darkness"* and nourish the *"wolf of light."* Anything you do not feed will eventually starve to death and die! That's the goal. We want to destroy and annihilate this evil, poisonous, ugly, and disastrous tongue. But how are we to accomplish this challenging feat? From my experience dealing with my unruly tongue, I have composed five ways we can feed the *"wolf of light."*

1. Commit and consecrate your heart, soul, and tongue daily to the Lord Jesus Christ.

> *"Through Him then, let us continually offer up a sacrifice of praise to God, that is, the fruit of lips (words) that give thanks to His name." (Heb. 13:15)*

This is a choice. When we *"choose"* to offer continual praise, we have sacrificed the ugliness of a *tainted tongue, slanderous speech, lewd language, gruesome gossip,* and *heinous hell.* Whatever words the mouth speaks, the heart follows.

> *"The good man out of the good treasure of his heart brings forth what is good, and the evil man out of the evil treasure brings forth what is evil; for his mouth speaks from that which fills his heart." (Luke 6:45)*

2. Practice and rehearse speaking words of encouragement and those that are empowering, edifying, and educating.

The objective is to speak life! Ephesians 4:29 wants us to practice and rehearse speaking life into the lives of others:

> *"Let no unwholesome word proceed from your mouth, but only such a word as is good for edification according to the need of the moment so that it will give grace to those who hear."*

To speak life is to release words that will *"stimulate"* spiritual growth and not *"stifle."* Paul wasn't talking to the unchurched. He was talking to the church. The church has the power to speak words that can change the universe. Ask yourselves. *"How can I use my words to build and not create a burden?* Which *"wolf* will I feed?"

3. Ask God to give you the wisdom, awareness, and cognizance of every word that comes from your mouth

This effort requires intentionality. God wants our words to be intentional, which means "boldness"! When the time comes for us to speak, speak to empower and encourage lives. When the time comes for us to remain silent, then do it intentionally, with the desire to edify and educate lives. Take responsibility and accountability for our words.

> *"The tongue is the only tool that gets sharper with use."*
> —Washington Irving

4. Approach the Father and ask for forgiveness of every unkind, unloving, and unfeeling word

> *"For we all stumble and sin in many ways. If anyone does not stumble in what he says [never saying the wrong thing], he is a perfect man [fully developed in character, without serious flaws], able to bridle his whole body and rein in his entire nature [taming his human faults and weaknesses]."* (James 3:2)

Contrary to popular belief, *"we all make plenty of mistakes!"* James wants to remind us, as well as himself, that no one is perfect, no one has it all together, and no one has said all the right things. Spending time alone with God is the foundation for repentance and asking for *"forgiveness"* for our words. Let's examine our words and begin to change the way we speak to demonstrate God's love for all humanity

5. **You are held responsible and held accountable for every word that comes from your mouth.**

> *"If anyone thinks himself to be religious, and yet does not bridle his tongue but deceives his own heart, this man's religion is worthless."* (James 1:26)

In this verse, James explains that religion is much more than hearing the word. Instead, it has less to do with information and more to do with the application. God wants us to act on His word and not just listen to it. There are many ways to apply the word. But the sure way is to *"bridle the tongue."* Believe it or not, we can do great work by *"putting some reins, restraints, and resistance on our tongue."*

> *"But prove yourselves doers of the word and not merely hearers who delude themselves. For if anyone is a hearer of the word and not a doer, he is like a man who looks at his natural face in a mirror; for once he has looked at himself and gone away, he has immediately forgotten what kind of person he was. But one who looks intently at the perfect law, the law of liberty, and abides by it, not having become a forgetful hearer but an effectual doer, this man will be blessed in what he does."* (James 1:22–25)

We should receive God's Word to the fullest so that our words come under His authority. Then, once we've heard it, we're responsible for acting, applying, and announcing it to the world. *This is doing!* We *act* by putting the word into action, *apply* it by practicing it in our lives, and finally *announce* His word in every corner of the earth. Acting, applying, and announcing take the Holy Spirit's leading.

> *"I fear we have many such in all congregations; admiring hearers, affectionate hearers, attached hearers, but all the while unblest, because they are nor doers of the word."*
>
> —Charles Spurgeon

To be responsible and accountable implies that God can count on us to wisely and carefully choose our words. We've all said something we wish we could retrieve and reverse. *This will not happen!* Our words are like a bullet discharged from the barrel of a gun. When the bullet is released, you cannot bring it back. Once the words have left our lips, we cannot recover them. They're gone! Thanks be to God! He offers us hope, help, and His word to teach us how to be responsible with our words.

> *"But each one must examine his own work, and then he will have reason for boasting in regard to himself alone, and not in regard to another. For each one will bear his own load."* (Gal. 6:4–5)

Imagine two young men who do not see eye to eye. One man did not use his words wisely and said inappropriate things about the other. Which man do you think took the responsibility to accept that his comments were inappropriate? We've read in Ephesians 4:29,

> *"Let no unwholesome word proceed from your mouth, but only such a word as is good for edification according to the need of the moment so that it will give grace to those who hear."*

In the preceding scenario, ask yourselves these questions.

1. "Did either man apply this verse to the situation?"
2. "Did their words edify the other, or did it tear them to shreds?"
3. "Did their words fulfill the other's need?"
4. "Will their words give grace to those who may have been privy to their situation?"

We can tame our tongue. However, we cannot do this in our own strength.

CONCLUSION

This year marks fifty years of teaching church music. I have worked with choirs, praise teams, bands, orchestras, and children's choirs. I've been honored to train, coach, and instruct countless singers, musicians, and children with extraordinary gifts, talents, and skills. Unfortunately, I've also encountered different personalities, attitudes, spirits, and behaviors. When confronted by a disgruntled musician, I realized my issue with an unruly tongue. This confrontation prompted me to pen *A Restless Evil*.

For the last ten years, I have had an overwhelming desire to write a book encouraging others to observe their tongue daily. I wrote *A Restless Evil* because I wasn't pleased with my *choice of words, and neither was God.* My breaking point was how I interacted with others and served in a ministry teaching capacity. Teaching has been one area in which God has gifted me and given me the passion, commitment, and duty to help the church grow and mature. When I decided to move forward with writing this book, I was encouraged to read James 3:1–2,

> *"Let not many of you become teachers, my brethren, knowing that as such we will incur a stricter judgment. For we all stumble in many ways. If anyone does not stumble in what he says, he is a perfect man, able to bridle the whole body as well."*

Yes, while teaching in the ministry, I stumbled in my speech. I have said unkind, unloving, and unpleasant things. And even now, I occasionally make flaws and omissions in my remarks, which I am not pleased. However, that does not disqualify me from being called by God to fulfill my purpose. Romans 11:29 says,

>"For the gifts and the calling of God are irrevocable."

This means God will never change His mind about what He has called us to do. If God has called us, the calling is still relevant, even in our "*stumbling*." James 3:2 says,

>"For we all stumble in many ways. If anyone does not stumble in what he says, he is a perfect man, able to bridle the whole body as well."

Whether or not I've said all the right or wrong things, God's calling is still in effect. And if God gave me the gift of teaching, if He gifted me in a specific area, the gift is still there!

The goal for you, me, and so many others is that we allow the Holy Spirit to teach us and guide us into all truth concerning our tongue and our words. Remember this:

>"Death and life are in the power of our tongue, And those who love it will eat its fruit." (Prov. 18:21).

THE END

Bibliography

Bible

Holy Bible: *New King James Version*, Review and Herald, 1998, Hagerstown, MD.

Peterson, Eugene H. *The Message*, NavPress, 2004, Carol Stream, IL.

New American Standard Bible, LaHabra, CA: Foundation Publications, for the Lockman Foundation, 1971, LaHabra, CA.

Siewert, Frances E. *The Amplified Bible*, Zondervan, 1958, Grand Rapids, MI.

Books and Quotes

Sermon, *"Two Sorts of Hearers,"* Charles Haddon Spurgeon, The Spurgeon Center, June 22, 2020: from *Metropolitan Tabernacle Pulpit*, volume 25.

Washington Irving Quotes: BrainyQuotes.com, BrainyMedia Inc. 2020, http:/www.brainy.com/quotes/Washington_irving_149282, accessed July 25, 2020.

"Figs and Olive Berries" by Charles Spurgeon, No. 3226, *Metropolitan Tabernacle*, Newington, September 11, 1879.

ABOUT THE AUTHOR

B orn in Monroe, Louisiana, Zachary Wayne Lavender migrated to Chicago, Illinois, and began his musical journey at the tender age of ten. Zachary's training was helmed by some of Chicago's finest in choral, church, and vocal music. In addition, he has done extensive training in voice pedagogy at Roosevelt University/Chicago Musical College under the guidance of Mr. Robert Long and Ms. Ruth Ann Bishop.

Throughout his fifty-year tenure as a church musician, Zachary has built a reputation for developing singers and musicians to perfect the church's music ministry. He is passionate about the needs and objectives of church music and the future generation of singers and musicians. He specializes in bringing the talent and gift of the musician to the forefront and allowing them to minister at their fullest capacity.

Zachary has continued to hone his skills as a composer, conductor, teacher, musician, and author. He counts it all joy, honor, and privilege to be chosen by God to help lead the church in music excellence and provide an avenue for those who desire to be whole and healed.

Mr. Lavender is the author of three books—"Victim of Circumstance," "In 5 Days," and An Audience of One-The Seriousness of Worship."

www.ingramcontent.com/pod-product-compliance
Lightning Source LLC
Chambersburg PA
CBHW072158060526
44654CB00046B/1341